Sharing mobility economy and social capital: BlaBlaCar creates relations just between heavy users?

di Mariachiara Montebello e Andrea Careddu

ABSTRACT

Our research concerns the car pooling service BlaBlaCar and the development of social and relational capital resulting from the usage of this platform.
The investigation is based particularly on the 2016 paper by Arcidiacono and Pais, which proves that most of BlaBlaCar users develop social relations with each other. Analyzing the methodology of the Arcidiacono and Pais paper we found out that they delivered the survey just to "heavy users" of BlaBlaCar (= people that used the service at least 5 times in a period of 4 months).
This is the starting point of our main research question: is the social relation development following the use of BlaBlaCar ordinary? Or does it just concern the heavy users of the service? If not, is the usage of BlaBlaCar correlated with other main reasons (above all, money saving)?

DATA SOURCES

The economic crisis encouraged new cultural practices and different production, distribution and consumption models based on reciprocity values, while the disintermediation offered by digital platforms lead to a better integration between economy and society. This cohesion resulted in in the affirmation of the sharing economy[1], which empowers consumers, that are now way more similar to producers (prosumer)[2].

It's also fair to say that we're currently living in the "trust era", since reputation and trust building systems are the main base of the collaborative economy[3]. Digital reputation can, in fact, promote virtuous behaviors[4], also thanks to the fear of the possible retaliations of other users[5].

Car pooling and BlaBlaCar

Car pooling popularity is growing thanks to the evolution of communication and geolocalization technologies, that made the user experience easier, immediate and safer than in the past (for example in terms of payment systems).

BlaBlaCar is a car pooling platform, also defined as a *"dynamic ride sharing"*[6], since it integrates technological innovations to offer unprofessional drivers the chance to share the car seats and the travel cost with other passengers. While these two categories of users gain an equal advantage in terms of money and time, they also create benefits for people unrelated to the service, reducing traffic, pollution and fuel consumption[7][8][9].

BlaBlaCar is one of the most successful sharing economy platforms and the largest community of car pooling in the world, with more than 35 million users in 22 countries around the globe. The firm retains about 8% of the ride fee and this is the only source of income, often reinvested in initiatives meant to encourage the community engagement.

---

[1] Pais, I. – Provasi, G. (2015), *Sharing economy: a step towards 're-embedding' the economy?*, in "Stato e Mercato", 105, 3, pp. 347-377
[2] Florida, R. (2002), *The Rise Of The Creative Class: And How It's Transforming Work, Leisure, Community And Everyday Life*, Basic Books, New York
[3] Mazzella, F. – Sandurarajan, A. (2016), *Entering the Trust Age*, BlaBlaCar & NYU-Stern, Parigi
[4] Arvidsson, A. – Peitersen, N. (2009), *The Ethical Economy*, http://www.ethicaleconomy.com/info/book
[5] Resnick, P. – Zeckhauser, R. (2002), *Trust Among Strangers in Internet Transactions: Empirical Analysis of eBay's Reputation System,* in M.R. Baye, "The Economics of the Internet and E-Commerce. Amsterdam", Elsevier Science, pp. 127-157
[6] Agatz, N. – Erera, A. – Savelsbergh, M. – Wang, X. (2012), *Optimization for dynamic ride-sharing: A review,* in "European Journal of Operational Research", 223, pp. 295–303
[7] Ferguson, E. (1997), *The rise and fall of the American carpool: 1970–1990*, in "Transportation", 24 (4), pp. 349–376
[8] Kelley, K.L. (2007), *Casual carpooling enhanced*, in "Journal of Public Transportation", 10 (4), pp. 119–130
[9] Chan, N.D. – Shaheen, S.A. (2012), *Ridesharing in North America: Past, Present, and Future*, in "Transport Reviews", 32:1, 93-112, DOI: 10.1080/01441647.2011.621557

In order to prevent a professional use, the platform imposes a limit for the refund requests based on the ACI official tariffs.

The trust building system consists in the subscription of a community agreement, while the reputational system is based on the acronym DREAMS: Declared (personal information), Rated (feedback and experience level), Engaged (ride reservation and prepayment), Active (information about the user's level of activity), Moderated (verified information), Social (integration with and links to the social network profiles of the users).

Previous researches

A research on the impact of this platform, conducted on more than 18 thousand users in 11 countries, highlighted a higher trust in BlaBlaCar (88%) than in work colleagues (58%) or neighbors (42%). Moreover, when compared to other platforms, BlaBlaCar reached +21% of trust, mainly thanks to the effectiveness of the feedback system.[10]

In the next pages we're going to focus on the Italian research by Arcidiacono and Pais. Summing up their results, we can say that they found out that the sharing economy is spreading among young people (aged 20-35) with a high level of instruction and good working conditions, that use BlaBlaCar for sentimental and recreational reasons.

The two researchers managed to define two main users profiles:
- Experienced travelers: men with a high school degree, that use the platform mostly as drivers, for reasons related to their job;
- Young explorers: younger and less experienced people that travel in their free time.

The main reasons why people use this platform seem to be the low price and the social aspects, despite a high remuneration of the users and the availability of means of transport.

BlaBlaCar users are more gregarious and trustful than the Italian average: the authors explained those characteristics proving the propensity of more than half of the users to travel together again. Indeed, only 20% of the users doesn't build any relationship while travelling with BlaBlaCar.

Analyzing the digital reputation tools, they found out that the rating and review systems are the main reasons why the users trust each other, even though they often trust the platform also when the users don't have any feedback yet. The same happens when they have to write negative reviews, since they usually try to compensate the bad aspects with positive elements.

The last part of the Arcidiacono and Pais research points out the sense of community felt by half of the interviewees, which usually talk about their BlaBlaCar experiences with their friends, family and other users, since they believe in the values and the philosophy of the service.

---

[10] Mazzella, F. – Sanduraralan, A. (2016), *Entering the Trust Age*, BlaBlaCar & NYU-Stern, Parigi

Despite most of the sample considers BlaBlaCar a community that helps changing our world, the main characteristic associated to the brand is still the comfort.[11]

---

[11] Arcidiacono, D. - Pais, I., *Reciprocità, fiducia e relazioni nei servizi di mobilità condivisa: un'analisi sul car pooling di BlaBlaCar*, Università Cattolica del Sacro Cuore, http://www.sisec.it/wp-content/uploads/2017/02/Arcidiacono-Pais-Car-pooling-bla-bla-car-full-paper-SISEC.pdf

RESEARCH QUESTION AND ANALYSIS TECHNIQUES

Analyzing the effects of BlaBlaCar on the social life of its users, we asked ourselves if the relevance of the social aspects of the platform was the same for heavy and less frequent users. We hypothesize that the majority of BlaBlaCar users, instead, prefer this platform because of the economic and practical advantages more than the sense of community. We choose to produce a quantitative research, delivering a survey (through Google Form) in which we used some of the questions adopted by Arcidiacono and Pais in their own project.

The research dimension that we considered were:
- Gender, age, educational level, work condition, income bracket and domicile of the user;
- Travel frequency, main role (driver or passenger), aims of the journeys;
- Values associated with BlaBlaCar and reasons why they use this platform;
- Relevance of the feedback system, trust placed in BlaBlaCar and in strangers in general;
- Social relations created as a consequence of the usage of the service;
- Sharing of information, stories and emotions linked to the BlaBlaCar experience;
- Emotional involvement in the community and opinions about this firm.

Using Microsoft Excel, we tried to correlate the results in order to observe if the ones obtained by Arcidiacono and Pais were similar or different when compared to ours.

DATA ANALYSIS

We managed to collect the answers of 429 BlaBlaCar users between 2018 May 30th and June 9th.

Socio demographic profile
Almost all of the users are young (90,9%), aged between 18 and 27 years (64,3%) and between 28 and 37 (26,6%). The adults (older than 38 years) are just the remaining 9,1% of the sample (4,9% between 38 and 47 years, 3,7% between 48 and 57 years, 0,5% more than 58 years).

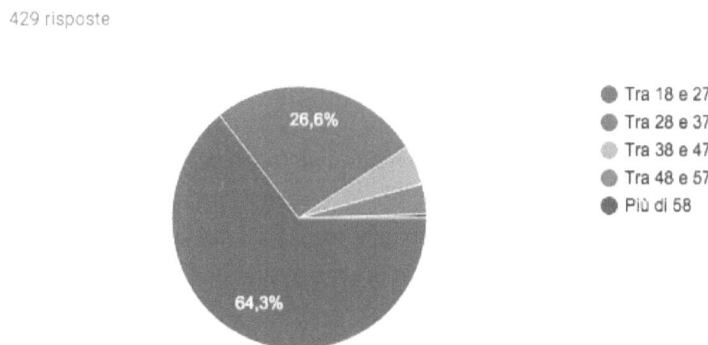

Graph no. 1 - Age of the surveyed

The majority of the interviewed is highly educated. 57,4% of the statistic sample has at least one degree: 28,2% has a degree, 23,8% a master's degree, 5,4% are (or have been) PhD students or got a university master.
41% of the surveyed attended high school, but 79% of them is attending university.
Just 1,6% of the respondent only attended the secondary school.

Titolo di studio (indicare il più elevato finora conseguito)
429 risposte

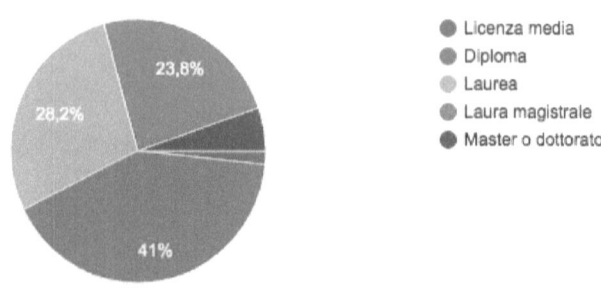

Graph no. 2 - Qualifications of the respondents

Our results about age and education confirm the Arcidiacono and Pais conclusion regarding sharing economy spreading more among young and well-educated people, known as Millennials or Y Generation.

Travel purposes
BlaBlaCar users can be divided in two almost equal groups: one (46,9%) uses the car pooling platform for ludic purposes (15,6% for holydays and pleasure trips and 31,2% to visit friends, family and partner), while the other group (51,7%) choose this service for professional and educational reasons (30,5% occasionally and 21,2% daily).
The remaining 1,4% of the sample use the platform in other ways (ex.: to reach airports badly connected to their hometown).

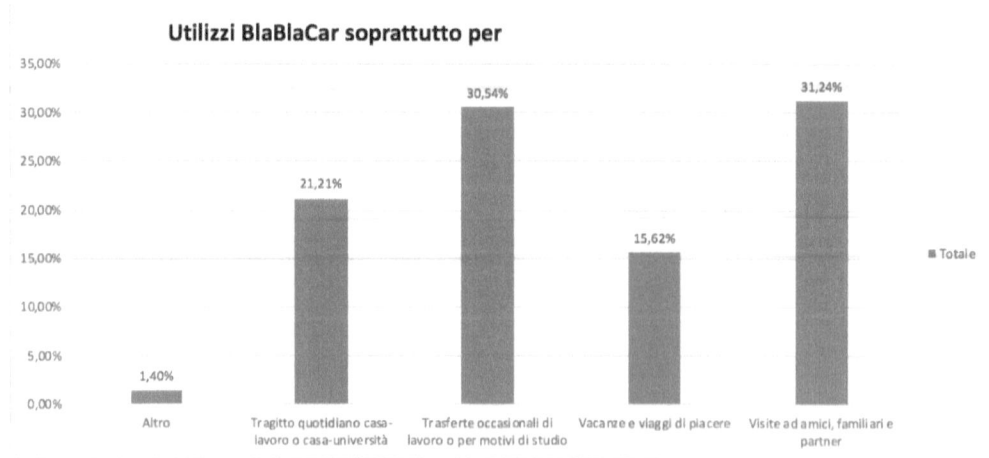

Graph no. 3 - Purposes of using BlaBlaCar

Comparing these data to the literature, we notice a bigger group of pleasure travelers (65%), that could be linked to the differences between the samples, as Arcidiacono and Pais studied the more active users with at least 5 travels with BlaBlaCar in the previous 4 months.
Our sample, instead, consists of people that travelled from 0 to more than 20 times in the last year.

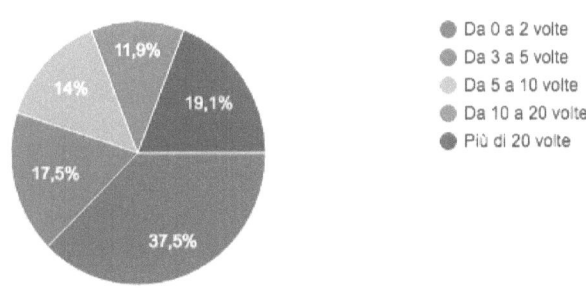

Graph no. 4 - Number of trips in the last year

We suppose that the reason of the difference between the two results could be that the more active users choose the platform more frequently for leisure trips because they're actually more used to travel for ludic purposes, since 4 out of 5 of the top users have a job, while in our sample the ratio is 1 out of 2.
In fact, from the Arcidiacono and Pais research resulted that 82% of reached users were workers. In our sample, instead, the most important percentage is represented by students (41%), followed by 4,2% of students looking for a job, 3,7% of unemployed looking for an occupation and 0,9% of unemployed. The half of the sample that has a job is composed by 28% of employees, 14% of working students, 8,2% of self-employed.

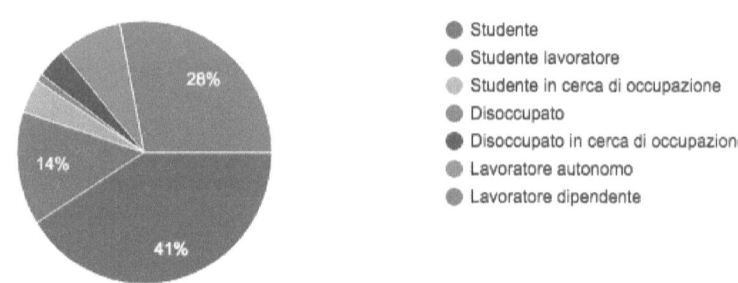

Graph no. 5 - Work condition of the sample

In order to understand the main reasons why people uses BlaBlaCar, we asked the users to assign from 1 to 7 points to the main aspects underlined by Arcidiacono and Pais. Saving money is clearly the main reason people use BlaBlaCar (with 1899 total points and an average of 4,4 in a range between 1 and 7), followed by comfort, that reached 1605 points in total with an average of 3,7 points (although 29,6% of the respondents consider it worthy of 3 points).

The lack of alternative means of transport is the third main reason why people use the platform, with an average of 3,2 points in a range between 1 and 7 (23,8% of the users gave 3 points to this reason) and a total score of 1411 points.

Travelling with company doesn't seem to be a significant reason to use BlaBlaCar, since it only scored 1246 points in total (averagely 2,9 out of 7), with the majority of the sample (52,9%) giving it only 1 or 2 points.

The same goes for environmental reasons, that only scored 1194 point and 2,8 on average, since 54,8% of the interviewed assigned 1 or 2 points out of 7.

Curiosity closes the chart, since "Discovering news ways to travel" was worthy of just 1 point for 39,4% of the users, thus reaching an average of 2,5 points and total score of 1061.

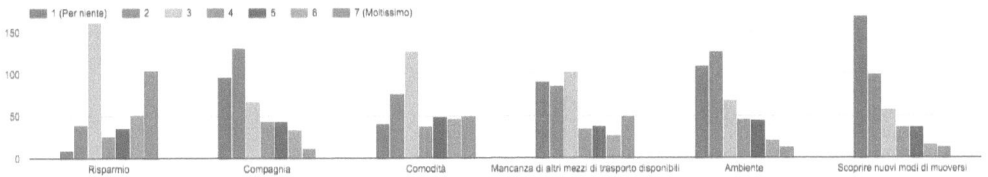

Graph no. 6 - Reasons why people choose to use BlaBlaCar

Comparing our results with the previous research we can say that while its characteristic of being cheap is still the main motivation to use BlaBlaCar, sociality is an aspect considered mainly by the more active users. Our research sample seems to be more influenced by practical motivations (saving money, comfort, lack of means of transport) than by the other benefits in terms of social experiences, environmental sustainability and curiosity.

We thought that the importance of the economic reasons could have been related to the high number of people (35,7%) that declared a very low income (less than 5000 euros per year).

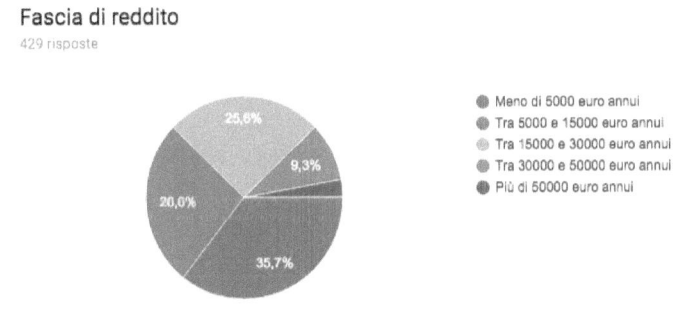

Graph no. 7 - Income brackets of the respondents

In fact, in our sample the bracket income seems to be related to the reasons why users choose to use BlaBlaCar and not more expensive means of transport, since the percentages of people that assigned just 1 point out of 7 to economic reasons gradually drops as the income bracket grows.

These data are deeply different from the one emerged from the Arcidiacono and Pais research, since the majority of their sample (62% of the passengers and 70,3% of the drivers) resulted to be satisfied by their economic situation, which explains why the economic reasons are not considered way more than the other aspects.

The results concerning the importance of the economic reasons could be also related to the gender of the respondents, since theirs were mostly men, that are generally paid more than women.[12]

Our sample, in fact, consist of the opposite groups: 71,6% female users and 28,4% male users.

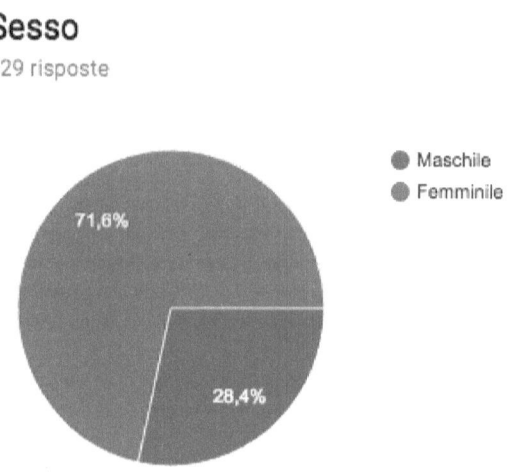

Graph no. 8 - Gender of the surveyed

This hypothesis turned out to be confirmed by the percentages of women that attributed the maximum score (7) to "Saving money", which is higher than the one of the men
On the contrary, the amount of men assigning only one point out of 7 to this attribute is twice the percentage of women.

Differences between male and female travelers
There are also a few more differences between male and female respondents.
- Despite having a low relevance in the research sample, company got the maximum score (in a scale from 1 to 7) by 4,9% of the male respondents and 1,9% of the female users.
- BlaBlaCar is considered a way to travel comfortably, by women (3,9 points on average) more than by men (3,4). These data are also reflected by the percentage

---

[12] Carlini, R. (2017) - *Perché le donne continuano a guadagnare meno degli uomini*, https://www.internazionale.it/opinione/roberta-carlini/2017/03/07/donne-guadagnano-meno-uomini

of men that gave comfort the minimum score (1), which is two times the one of women. in reverse, the number of women that gave the maximum value (7) to this attribute is twice the amount of men.
- Another reason to choose BlaBlaCar that presents significant differences depending on the gender of the interviewees is the lack of alternative transport means. On average, this is a reason to choose the car pooling service worthy 2,9 points out 7 for men and 3,4 for women. Those data could be related to some Italian women characteristics. In fact, it's commonly agreed that in Italy many women don't personally drive for long distances and to feel less secure using public transports for their travels. Indeed, we noticed a regular trend in the values for this attribute, with women giving a growing importance to the lack of alternatives and men assigning a decreasing value. This assumption can be (at least partially) supported by the difference existing between the percentages of male and female passengers and drivers, with 82,41% of the female respondent and 65,57% of the male ones being passengers, while male drivers are twice the female ones.

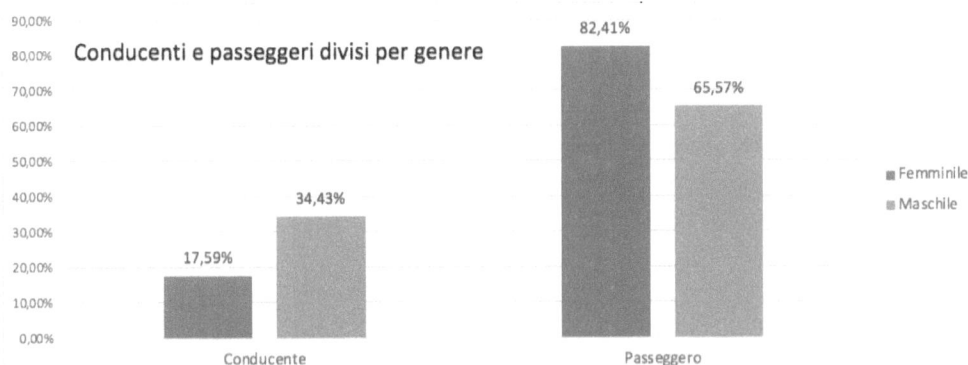

Graph no. 9 - Gender of drivers and passengers

Differences between drivers and passengers
- Comparing the average points given by passengers and drivers, we notice that company is more important for drivers, since they gave an average of 3,3 points (in a scale from 1 to 7) to this aspect and only 11,5% of them assigned just one point, while passengers gave an average of 2,8 points and 25,5% of them only assigned it one point. This result can be linked to a stronger confidence in driving next to someone than in doing it alone, which results proved to be felt by the older users.
- Comfort is more popular among the passengers than the drivers. In fact, we noticed that the majority of drivers (42,7%) only assigned it 1 or 2 points, while only 23,1% of the passengers did the same. The amount of passengers that gave 6 or 7 points to this value (25,5%) is also twice the drivers percentage (12,5%). This

result is probably linked to the less stress obviously implied by not having the responsibility of driving a car.
- Similar data emerged from the analysis of the lack of means of transport, that got 1 point from 33,3% of the drivers and 17,8% of the passengers, while 13,5% of the passengers and only 5,21% of the drivers gave it the maximum score (7). This problem seems also to affect more south Italy and the islands, where the percentages of users giving 7 points to the lack of means of transport are of 17,6% of the South surveyed and 19,5% of the respondents living in the islands (against 7,1% of the central Italy interviewees and 9,7% of the north ones).
- Still, saving money is clearly the main reason why all users choose BlaBlaCar, since only 9 out of 429 surveyed gave it only 1 point, 6 passengers and 3 drivers. Passengers are probably more interested in economic reasons because they are mainly students (49%), followed by employees (22,5%), working students (12,6%), self-employed (5,7%), students looking for a job (5,4%), unemployed looking for an occupation (3,9%) and unemployed (0,9%). A different situation results about drivers: they are mostly employees (46,9%), followed by working students (18,7%), self-employed (16,7%), students (13,5%), unemployed looking for a job (3,1%) and in the end unemployed (1%).

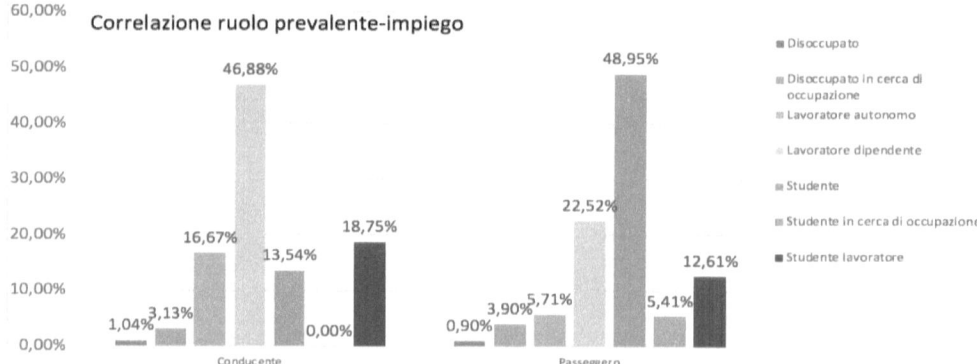

Graph no. 10 - Correlation between main role (driver or passenger) and occupation

The popularity of the economic reason and of the lack of means of transport can be also explained by another result: since the majority of the BlaBlaCar users interviewed consists of students (59,2%) and 64,3% of the sample is aged between 18 and 27 years old, it's possible that a large part of the sample hasn't got a car (or even a driving license) or still occasionally borrows one from their parents, thus feeling more forced to rely on public transports and sharing platforms.

165 out of 429 surveyed are, in fact, students (currently not working or looking for an occupation) aged between 18 and 27 years old.

Through a deeper analysis we actually found out that 47,87% of those 165 people assigned a high score (5-7) to "Saving money" and 93,94% of them uses BlaBlaCar more as passengers.
This would explain why the whole research sample is divided in a 77,6% of respondents that uses the platform mostly as a passenger and a way smaller group of users (22,4%) that drives the car.

Utilizzi maggiormente BlaBlaCar come:
429 risposte

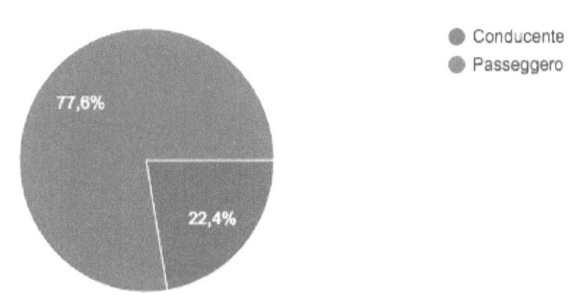

Graph no. 11 - Main role of the surveyed (driver or passenger)

Social relations
In this next section, we'll try to understand if users really develop any kind of social relation with people they met using BlaBlaCar.
We started asking if they ever met their partner on platform and 98,3% of them answered "No" (although 7 of the interviewees said that they actually met their partner, current or ex, using BlaBlaCar!). 38% of our sample said that they became friends on social media platforms with people they met using the car pooling service, while 85% never build any friendship with other users and 87,1% hasn't programmed any activities (ex.: dinners, travels) together. Out of 10 users, only 4 follow each other on social network and 1 actually builds a friendship with another user or shares other experiences outside the platform with him/her.
However, we notice that the majority of our sample (59,7%) travelled again using BlaBlaCar with people met on platform.

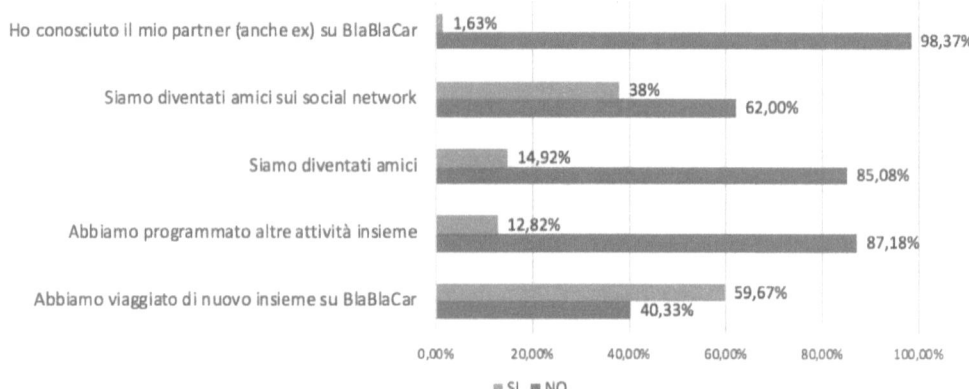

Graph no. 12 - Social contact kept by BlaBlaCar users with each other

Therefore, our conclusion is that it's really unusual to establish any kind of social relation out of the platform, since the only positive index is related to other journeys that the users shared via BlaBlaCar.

These last data may seem to underline the level of trust on the platform, allowing us to point that the users refuse unfair practices, like exchanging their telephone numbers or adding each other on social media to plan future travels privately and thus save the commission fee. Users prove that they consider the service fares right, but we have to consider that part of this behavior is due to BlaBlaCar preventing a professional usage of the platform, establishing a fare limit for every km traveled.

Review and rating
The trust placed in the platform is confirmed by the high percentage of users (64,3%) that trust each other thanks to the possibility to read the feedbacks received on the profile, followed by another 20,5% that has faith in BlaBlaCar security systems.
10,5% of the sample trusts people that uses this kind of platforms, while only 4,7% trusts strangers in general.

Accetti di viaggiare con sconosciuti soprattutto perché ...
429 risposte

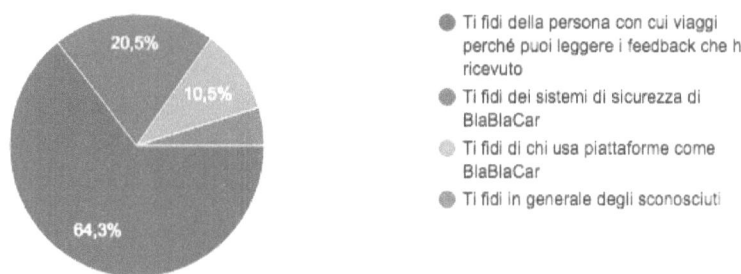

Graph no. 13 - Reasons why the sample travels with unknown people

This partition is valid for both drivers and passengers. There's also a small amount (around 6%) of passengers more confident in the feedback system than the drivers, which have a little more faith in strangers.
We hypothesized that this result could be related to the age and the experience level of the users.

- Regarding the age of the respondents, both drivers and passengers seem to rely mostly on the feedback system up to 47 years old, but then open themselves to unknown people and to the users of sharing economy platforms.
- As of the experience level of the surveyed, the feedback system appears to be the first choice of more and less frequent travelers, always followed by the trust placed in BlaBlaCar's security systems. This last element resulted to be more appreciated by the less experienced users, which may obviously be more hesitant to trust unknown people.

The feedback system
When asked about their behavior before a journey, most of the interviewees of all categories admit they usually examine the profiles and then choose who to travel with (66,7%).
27,7% of the surveyed takes a look at the profiles, but then travels with everyone, while only 24 people (5,6%) doesn't even look at the accounts of the other users and accept them anyway.

Prima del viaggio ...
429 risposte

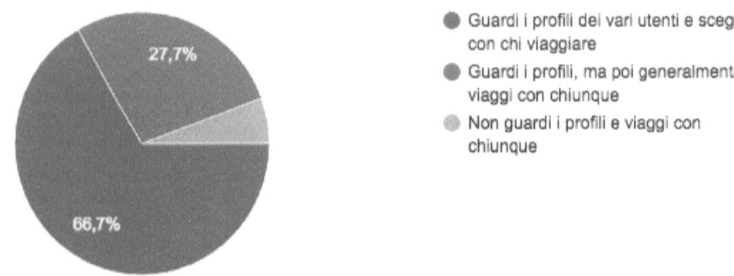

Graph no. 14 - Behaviors concerning the profiles of the users before the trip

In the Arcidiacono and Pais research, people were distributed in the 3 categories in a more uniform way, while in our research the group that checks the profiles and decides who to travel with is almost always twice the others.
As those researchers did, we crossed the two questions about the reasons why users accept to travel with unknown people and what they do before a trip.
The results confirmed a low generalized confidence.
As a matter of fact, going deeper into the different categories, we can see that the previous division of the sample is pretty similar to the one existing in the specific groups:
- Most of the people who trust the security systems of BlaBlaCar (62,5%) tends to be cautious and check the profile of users before sending or accepting the request, while 30,7% checks it but then travels with everyone and 6,8% doesn't even look at the profile before asking or accepting the passage.
- The same happens among the group that trust other users thanks to the feedbacks, with the highest percentage of people that only accept to travel with other users once checked their profile (71%), while 27,9% looks at it but doesn't really consider their information and only 3 people (1,1%) doesn't look at the user's profile at all.
- A similar situation concerns the ones that trust people that use platforms like BlaBlaCar, but with a higher percentage of respondents that doesn't take a look at the profiles (17,8%) of the users. People that check but then ignore them represent 20% of the sample and 62,2% chose who to travel with just after looking at the accounts.
- The only different situation is the one of the users that trust strangers in general. In the Arcidiacono and Pais research the group that generally trusts unknown people had the lowest rate of respondent choosing who to travel with by reading

their feedbacks, so it was fair to conclude that who trusts unknown people in general tends to don't really care about the ratings of the users. However, our group is more heterogeneous, with almost equal percentages of people who choose their travel mates only after looking at their feedbacks (35%), people that look at their profiles but aren't really selective (30%), and people who don't even look at the accounts and travel with everyone (35%). Still, as predictable, this last group of users has the highest number of trustful people in our sample too, but while from the Arcidiacono and Pais survey resulted a significant correlation between people that generally trust strangers and the ones that look the profiles but then travel with everyone, from our survey there are two other groups that have the same level of trust. In fact, we notice that the percentage of people that check the accounts of the users but then are not selective are quite the same among the ones that trust the security of the platform (30,6%), the group that trust people because they can read their feedbacks (27,9%) and people that generally trust the unknown (30%). We think that in our sample, more populated by occasional users, some people seem to be incoherent, declaring that they generally trust strangers, but then being selective with BlaBlaCar users.

The low generalized trust is also proved by the question about whether travelling or not with a user that hasn't got any feedback yet.

Indeed, 57,3% of the respondents admit that they would accept to travel with him/her only after a few messages exchanged and 25,9% of the interviewees reject the idea to travel with a user without feedback. Only 16,8% would travel with them anyway.

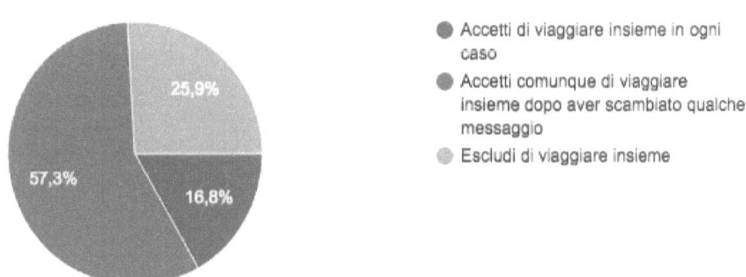

Graph no. 15 - Behaviors towards users without feedbacks

Our results are once again very different from the ones of Arcidiacono and Pais, that had a higher percentage of people that would travel with users without feedbacks after some message exchanges (73%), a considerable lower percentage of people that would have

avoided this hypothesis (5,9%) and a higher number of interviewed that would have travelled with them anyway (21,1%).
This is another situation which could be explained by the lower amount of experience of our sample, compared to the one of the previous research. We supposed that more expert users of BlaBlaCar trust the platform enough to be willing to accept more frequently to share their travels with users with no feedbacks.

- We tried to verify this correlation and, although the habit of exchanging a few messages before accepting to travel together is widespread in all the ranges, obviously less frequent travelers (0-5 times a year) are less inclined to accept to travel with people without feedbacks and 30,43% of occasional users (0-2 trips a year) excludes this possibility, more than expert surveyed.
- However, 20,45% of the users that in the previous question said that they trust BlaBlaCar security system, now excludes the possibility to travel with someone who doesn't have any feedback yet. This result proves once again the insecurities people feels in trusting unknown people without a proof of their responsibility and correctness.

These feelings lead people to be honest when they have the chance to express their opinion.
Indeed, when asked about what they would do after an unpleasant experience, the majority of our sample (53,8%) admit they would leave a negative feedback.
39,9% of the users chose to don't leave any feedback at all, but only 6,3% of the users would rather leave a positive feedback in order to preserve the user's reputation.

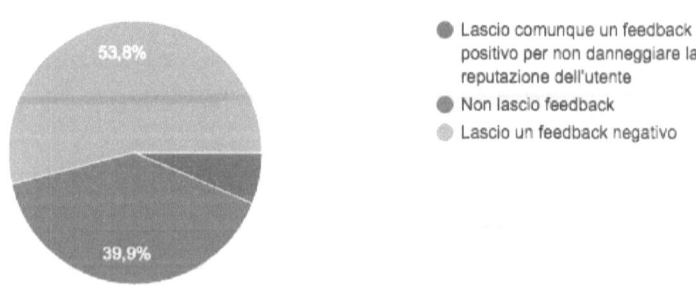

Graph no. 16 - Behaviors towards other users after an unpleasant experience

Those results are quite similar to the ones obtained by Arcidiacono and Pais, but in their research the percentage of people giving a negative feedback was way higher.

We assume that our users, travelling less frequently, don't really care about the rating and reviewing system, since they don't really see BlaBlaCar as a community, but just a simple mean of transport they can use when they need to.

The BlaBlaCar network

In order to understand the level of the sense of membership in the community, we asked a few more question already proposed by Arcidiacono and Pais.
The first one is about the habit of sharing information, stories and emotions linked to the BlaBlaCar experiences.
Our sample happened to have shared their thoughts mostly (87,9%) with their friends, more than with their parents (70,9%) and other BlaBlaCar users (69,7%). Only 1 out 5 (20,7%) of the surveyed shared their experiences on social media or messaging apps and 1 out of 10 never shared any of his emotions.

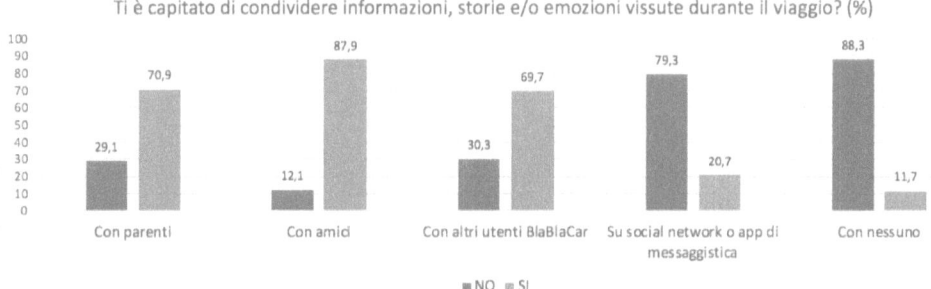

Graph no. 17 - Ways people share their BlaBlaCar experiences

Comparing our results with the ones obtained by Arcidiacono and Pais, we notice their higher percentage of people that shared their experiences with other BlaBlaCar users, meaning that the more experienced travelers usually talk about the service with other users, while our sample could be considered more populated by potential ambassadors of the platform, since they prefer to talk with friends (87,9%) and family (70,9%).
However, our surveyed are more willing to not share any of their experiences with anybody, with twice the percentage of "no" obtained in the Arcidiacono and Pais sample. Nevertheless, while Arcidiacono and Pais presented the option "Nobody, ever", we just wrote "With nobody", so we can't be sure that the users answered to this question thinking about all their experiences (of which they could have shared some o none) or if they could have answered "Yes" thinking about one or many travel they did not talk about with anyone, but at the same time answered "No" to the other options, referring to experiences they shared with someone. Since the percentage is low we assume that almost all the interviewees that answered "Yes" to the last option answered "No" at the previous ones.

What is BlaBlaCar?

Afterwards, we proposed an explicit question about the characteristic associated to BlaBlaCar.

Despite being less frequent users of the platform, our respondents are way more involved in the philosophy and the values of the firm, since our percentage (94,41%) is twice the one reached by the Arcidiacono and Pais (44,4%). The same goes for the sense of belonging to the community, felt more by our sample (57,34%) than from their interviewed (44,3%). However, a big distance between the two results is reached also with the question about the comfort, with 98,14% of our sample and 61,5% of their one agreeing with the sentence.

Nevertheless, the percentage of respondents that answered "No" to those questions grows with the involvement in the community that the sentences imply, starting from 1,86% not labeling the service as comfortable and ending up with 42,66% not feeling part of the community.

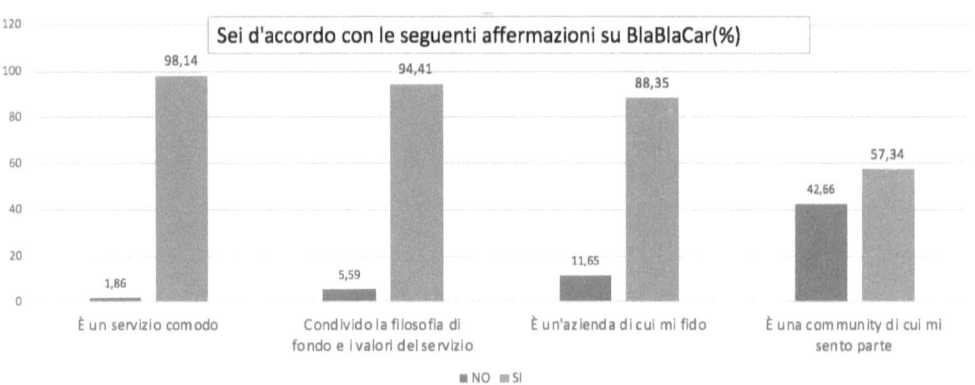

Graph no. 18 - Definitions of BlaBlaCar

Despite these results, our survey points out that 88,8% of the people who defined BlaBlaCar as a comfortable service also said that the platform is a company in which they trust, just like the Arcidiacono and Pais research does.

Now we can see if there are any correlations between the community membership perceived by the users and the behavior of the respondents after a bad experience with BlaBlaCar. We analyzed the answers of those that considered themselves being a part of the BlaBlaCar community and we noticed that they are more inclined (56,1%) to leave a negative feedback than the group that answered "No", although half of the latter would do the same. The percentage of surveyed that would rather not leave any feedback is indeed higher among those that don't really feel part of the community, proving that they don't really care about the welfare of the users and the reliability of the platform because they only use it for practical purposes.

The BlaBlaCar community

The last question is meant to get to know more about the level of membership felt by the users interviewed.

We asked them how much, in a scale from 1 to 7, they feel part of a community which helps changing the world for the better (providing a new way of using planet's resources and recapture trust between people).

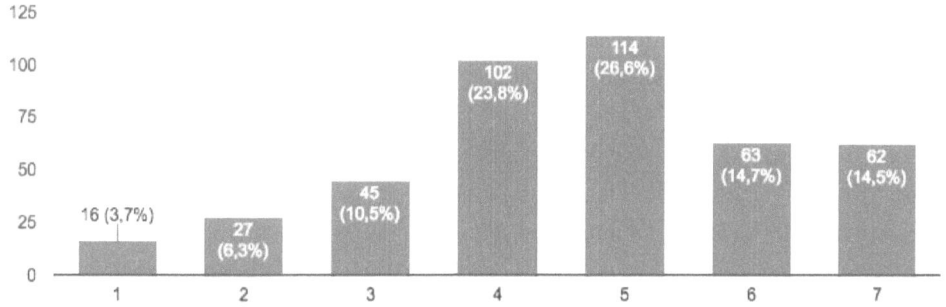

In quanto utente BlaBlaCar, quanto ti senti parte di una comunità che sta contribuendo a cambiare in positivo il m...uista della fiducia tra persone, ecc.)?
429 risposte

Graph no. 19 - Level of community membership felt by the users

Arcidiacono and Pais managed to reach an 85% of users that feel a fairly or highly sense of belonging to the BlaBlaCar community, while only 55,8% of our respondents said the same (assigning from 5 to 7 points).

From these it results that 5 is the most popular answer and 4,65 out of 7 is the average value.

CONCLUSIONS

All the data we collected lead us to the main conclusion that, while the BlaBlaCar heavy users interviewed by Arcidiacono and Pais feel more involved in the social consequences and the immaterial values linked to the platform, the less experienced users have a way more practical consideration of the service, of which they consider mainly the economic and useful characteristics.
However, it's important to underline that our sample was defined casually, while the previous research was conducted considering data provided by BlaBlaCar itself.
Our research may also overlook other reasons (like, for example, comfort, ecology and flexibility) that may have the same influence as the social aspects (or even more) on the users, when it comes to choose between platforms like BlaBlaCar and more classic means of transport. In the question concerning the reasons why the users choose the platform, we put the option "Comfort", which in Italian is "Comodità", that could be read as comfort of the car itself but also as flexibility in terms of time and place. These two dimensions could have been separated or explained in a better way.
Considering these aspects, this study can be a starting point for future investigations about the role of social relations in other services and platforms that are emerging thanks as the sharing economy spreads, like Uber, AirBnb, Couchsurfing.
We also left out a few possible options in the registry section. We didn't offer the option "Retired" in the question about the job, but since the older people generally don't use those online platforms and many of them aren't confident in travelling with strangers or don't even drive anymore, we don't think this omission would have affected our results so much.
Speaking about the place of residence of our surveyed, the majority lives in Northern Italy (45,5%), followed by Central Italy (26,3%) and the islands (20,3%), while only 34 out of 429 respondents (7,9%) come from the South. We correlated those results to the higher presence and organizational level of the means of transport in the Northern area, but it's also possible that the results were influenced by the fact that who made this survey lives in Milan and comes from Abruzzo (Central Italy) and Sardinia (Island). As a consequence, it's possible that the survey was reached more by people that live in those regions. It could be interesting to repeat the survey with a more homogeneous and significative sample, in order to portray the differences between those areas.
The same goes for the age of the respondents, since who conducted this research is aged between 23 and 25 years, so it's possible that we reached more easily young people, especially university students. So it could be useful to repeat the research with a more balanced breakdown by age.

www.ingramcontent.com/pod-product-compliance
Lightning Source LLC
Chambersburg PA
CBHW031942170526
45157CB00008B/3281